Patient Name
Address YOUR
Date

Rx

for

HEALING

MD WORD OF GOD
Signature Jesus

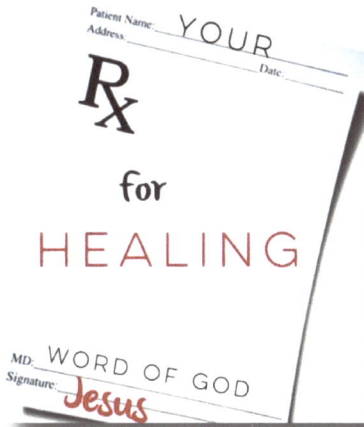

A journey to wholeness:
mind, body and soul.
Live Restored through
the Word of God.

Michelle Bollom

Introduction

The Promises in the Bible are God Breathed. 2 Timothy 3:16 MSG
Every part of Scripture is God-breathed and useful one way or another—showing us truth, exposing our rebellion, correcting our mistakes, training us to live God's way. Through the Word we are put together and shaped up for the tasks God has for us.

The Word is what started it all. The Word was God from day one. John 1:1-5 MSG
The Word was first, the Word present to God, God present to the Word. The Word was God, in readiness for God from day one. Everything was created through him; nothing—not one thing! -came into being without him. What came into existence was Life, and the Life was Light to live by. The Life-Light blazed out of the darkness; the darkness couldn't put it out.

The Word became flesh and dwells among us. John 1:14 ESV
And the Word became flesh and dwelt among us, and we have seen His glory, glory as of the only Son from the Father, full of grace and truth.

God forgives, God heals, God redeems, God renews and restores. Psalm 103:3-5 MSG He forgives your sins—every one. He heals your diseases—every one. He redeems you from hell—saves your life! He crowns you with love and mercy—a paradise crown. He wraps you in goodness—beauty eternal. He renews your youth—you're always young in his presence.

After suffering a stroke in 2008, I took to God's Word. I was so overwhelmed with multiple medications and diagnosis that I could barely function. The enemy likes to convince us that we will always stay sick and defeated. I believe that God can work through doctors and medications, but I am living proof and firmly believe that God's will is to heal us and that the Great Physician wants us to seek His promises for our healing too.

My prayer for you:

Beloved, I pray that in every way you may succeed and prosper and be in good health physically, just as I know your soul prospers spiritually. ~3 John 1:2

In the book of Matthew we read that Jesus went throughout Galilee…. *healing every disease and every affliction* among the people.

And Jesus went throughout all Galilee, teaching in their synagogues and proclaiming the gospel of the kingdom and healing every disease and every affliction among the people.
~ Matthew 4:23

God's will is still the same today. He wants to heal every disease and every affliction among His people.

If these Bible verses are not enough to convince you that there is tremendous power in the Word of God, I hope to convince you as you take a journey with me for the next month on what I call your Rx for Healing.

Come, and see the victories of the cross. Christ's wounds are thy healings, His agonies thy repose, His conflicts thy conquests, His groans thy songs, His pains thine ease, His shame thy glory, His death thy life, His sufferings thy salvation.
~Matthew Henry

Healing power is at work in me.
The Word of God is life to me.
It is medicine, healing, and health to all my flesh.
Healing power is at work in me!
~Keith Moore
God's Will to Heal

<u>One</u>

I must serve the Lord my God. If I do this, God will take away all sickness from me. ~Exodus 23:25 ERV

Lord, help me to break my selfishness and self-serving tendencies to fully serve You. Help me to serve others in my waiting. Remove my focus off my sickness to focus on You and Your will. Thank You for the promise to take all sickness away from me.

<u>Two</u>

Heal me, Lord, and I'll be healed. Save me and I'll be saved, for You are my heart's desire.
~Jeremiah 17:14 CEB

Lord, when I sometimes start to desire counterfeits to comfort me, remind me that nothing promises to heal or save me but You. My heart's desire is for only You.

<u>Three</u>

God will heal and mend me. God will make me whole and bless me with an abundance of peace and security. ~Jeremiah 33:6 CEB

Thank You Lord that Your promise is to make me not only whole, but also to bless me with peace and security. Heal and mend me Lord. I am Yours!

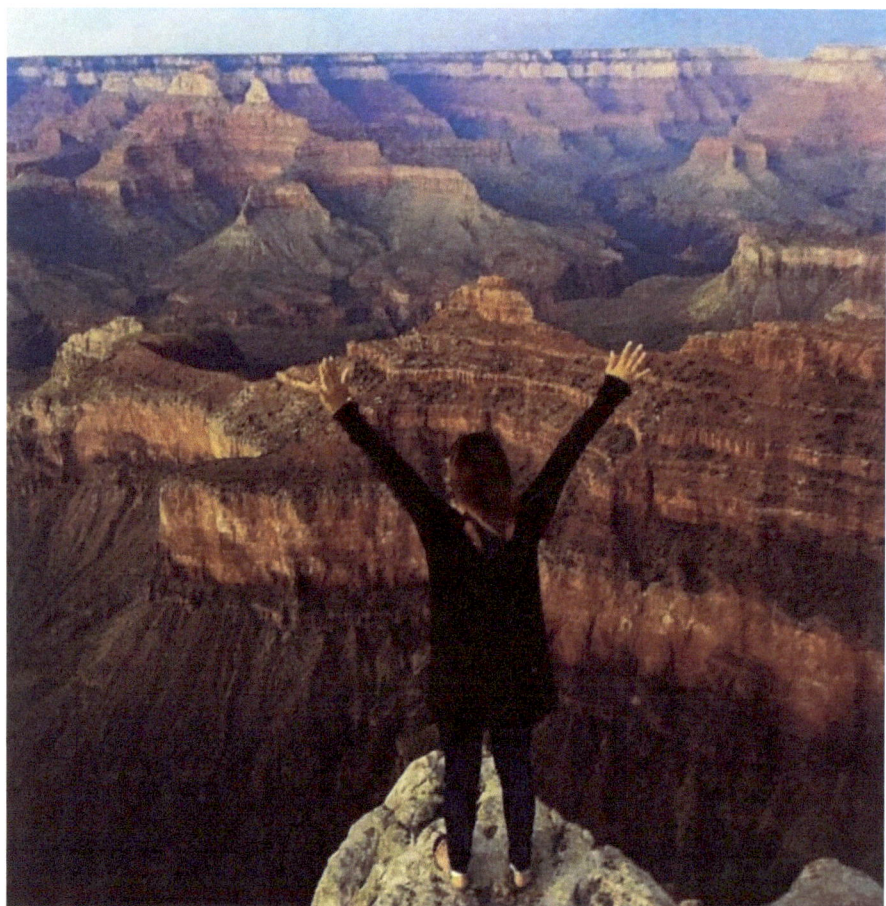

<u>Four</u>

Whatever I pray for or ask from God, I believe that I will receive it and I will.
~Mark 11:24 VOICE

Lord, some days the enemy will get my mind swirling with doubt. Clear away all unbelief from me. Hear my prayers, I believe You will answer me and know that You will supply for all my needs.

<u>Five</u>

My faith has healed me. I go in peace and am free from my sickness. ~Mark 5:34 NLV

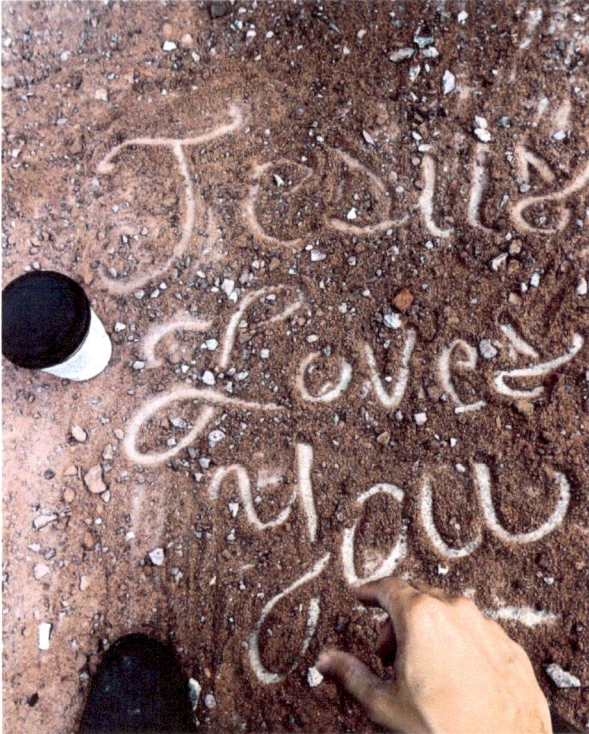

Your Word says that Faith as small as a mustard seed is all I need. Lord, today, I declare that my faith has healed me! I will go about my day in peace, free from sickness.

<u>Six</u>

I keep God's words before me; I meditate on them; I set them safely in my heart, for they are life. They bring wholeness and healing to my body.
~Proverbs 4:21-22 VOICE

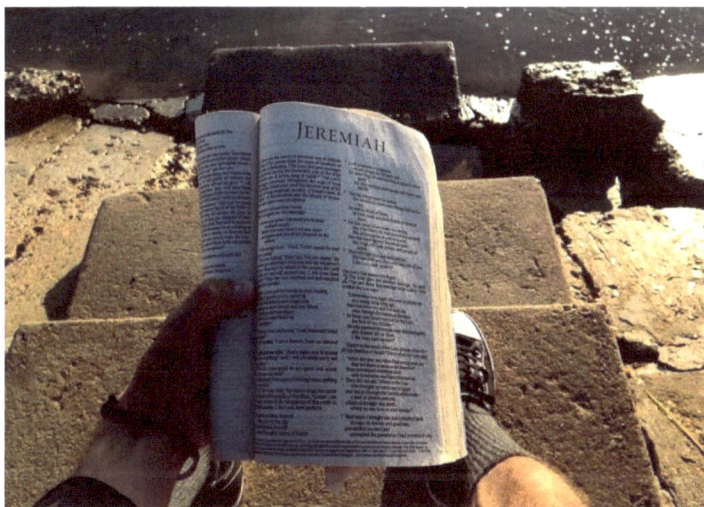

Lord, only You can promise me wholeness and healing. Your will is to heal me and Your Word is life to me. I keep Your Words always before me and meditate on them as I set them safely upon my heart.

<u>Seven</u>

Pleasant words are like a honeycomb; sweet and delightful to my soul and healing to my body.
~Proverbs 16:24 AMP

Lord, help to guard the words that come from my mouth. May I speak life, health, and hope so that my soul is delighted and my body is healed.

<u>Eight</u>

A cheerful disposition is good for my health; gloom and doom leave me bone-tired.
~Proverbs 17:22 MSG

Lord, remove my gloom and doom outlook and refresh and restore my soul. I choose *joy* today! I choose to have a cheerful disposition.

<u>Nine</u>

I belong to God. So I have won the victory. The One who is in me is greater than the one who is in the world.
~1 John 4:4 GW

Sickness is not greater than my God. I belong to God so I have won the victory over sickness. My God is within me and I will be healed.

<u>Ten</u>

And I am sure of this; God will listen to me whenever I ask Him for anything in line with His will.
~1 John 5:14-15 TLB

My cries never fall on deaf ears. Lord, thank You that You always listen to me when I cry out to You. Show me Your perfect will for me. Help me to also listen so that I can come into alignment with Your will.

<u>Eleven</u>

I come to Jesus when I am weary and burdened, and He gives me rest.
~Matthew 11:28 NIV

Lord, I am tired. I am weary and worn out and needing Your perfect rest. I come to You surrendered; ready to have You remove all of my weariness and burdens.

<u>Twelve</u>

I do not fear, for it is the Lord my God who is fighting for me.
~Deuteronomy 3:22 AMP

When others are ready to give up, You never do. When I am ready to give up Lord, You never do. Thank You that I always have You in my corner fighting for me. I will not fear any diagnosis, pain, or problems today. I will let You fight for me.

<u>Thirteen</u>

The Lord will remove all sickness from me.
~Deuteronomy 7:15 HCSB

Thank You Lord that ALL means ALL…
Not just the easy, the convenient, nor the small or insignificant. The big, the bad, the inconvenient, are nothing for You to remove. You remove all sickness from me.

Fourteen

Christ himself bore my sins in His body on the tree- that I might die to sin and live to righteousness. By His wounds I have been healed.
~1 Peter 2:24 ESV

Lord, what a sacrifice You made for me to live in righteousness and be healed. When my wounds feel like they will never heal, reassure me that the wounds You suffered on my behalf on the tree of Calvary includes all my wounds being healed.

Fifteen

Christ was pierced for my transgressions; He was crushed for my iniquities; upon Him was the chastisement that brought me peace, and with His wounds I am healed.
~Isaiah 53:5 ESV

The chastisement that was placed upon You brought me peace and healing. Lord I can't grasp the magnitude of Your suffering when my suffering seems so small in comparison to what You had to endure. Lord, help me to never take for granted that the removing of my transgressions and iniquities cost You greatly. Thank You for deeming me worthy of such a gift.

<u>Sixteen</u>

Because I trust in God the Eternal One I will regain my strength. I will soar on wings as eagles. I will run—never winded, never weary. I will walk—never tired, never faint. ~Isaiah 40:31 VOICE

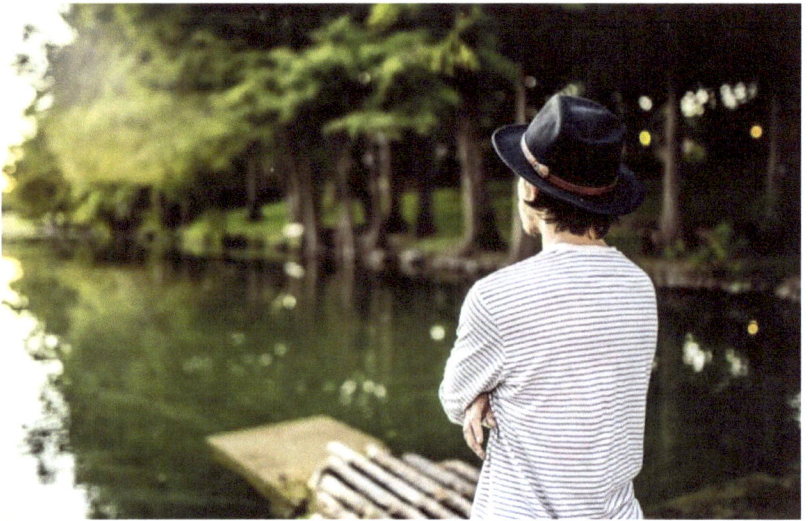

Lord, regain my strength. Help me to run and not be winded or weary. I will walk in strength and never tire or faint because You, God, the Eternal One, whom I place my trust in, live within me.

Seventeen

O Lord, your discipline is good
and leads to life and health. Oh,
heal me and make me live!
~Isaiah 38:16 TLB

Lord, thank You that when You
discipline and correct me it always
leads to life, health and my
ultimate good. You not only heal
me and make me live, but You
lovingly discipline me when
needed.

Eighteen

O Lord my God, I cried to You for help, and You have healed me.
~Psalm 30:2 AMP

Through my tears and cries Lord, You hear me. You are always there to help and to heal me.

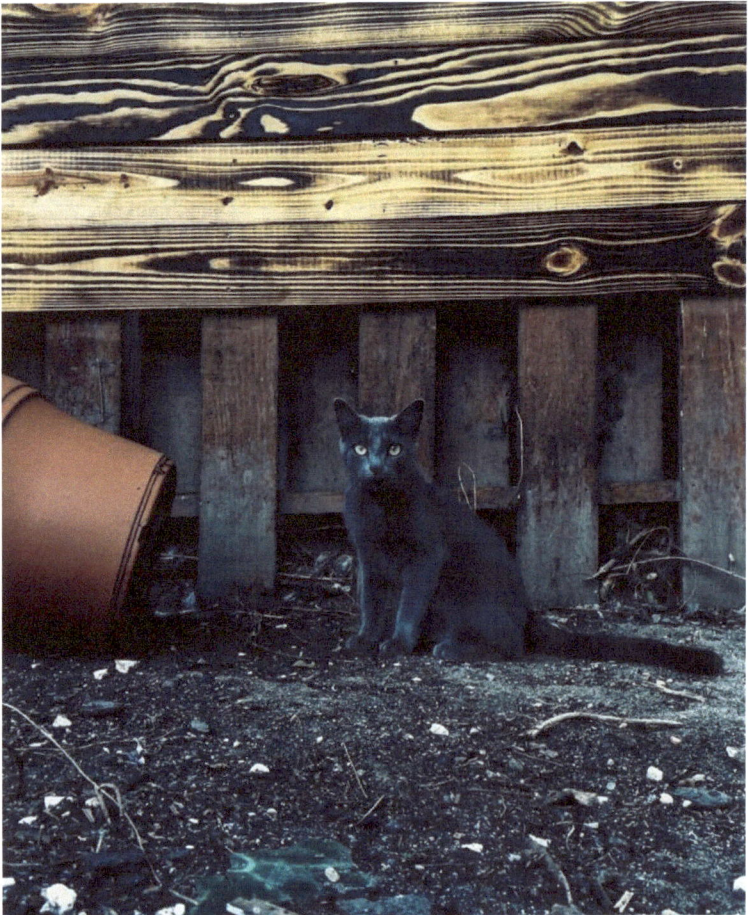

<u>Nineteen</u>

God keeps me from all evil and preserves my life. He keeps His eye upon me as I come and go and always guards me.
~Psalm 121:7-8 TLB

Thank you Lord for loving me so much that despite my shortcomings You still promise to guard over me in my coming and goings. Thank You that You keep me from all evil and preserve my life.

Twenty

I won't die—No! I will live and declare what the Lord has done.

~Psalm 118:17 CEB

The enemy will not have me. I will not die! I will live and declare all that the Lord has done for me.

<u>Twenty-One</u>

God sent out His Word and healed me, snatching me from the door of death.
~Psalm 107:20 NLT

Your Word heals me Lord. Thank You for rescuing me from the door of death. Thank You that all Your promises are Yes and Amen.

<u>Twenty-Two</u>

The Lord will sustain and strengthen me on my sickbed; in my illness, God will restore me to health.
~Psalm 41:3 AMP

Lord, I thank You that you sustain and strengthen me through sickness. Thank you that You will restore me back to health and wholeness.

<u>Twenty-Three</u>

God is the healer of the brokenhearted. He is the one who bandages my wounds.
~Psalm 147:3 GW

Lord, sometimes wounds are not visible to others, but they are always visible to You. Thank You for being my healer, repairer of my broken heart and bandaging up all my wounds.

<u>Twenty-Four</u>

Praise Yahweh, my soul, and never forget all the good He has done: He is the One who forgives all my sins, the One who heals all my diseases, the One who rescues my life from the pit, the One who crowns me with mercy and compassion, the One who fills my life with blessings so that I become young again like an eagle.
~Psalm 103:2-5 NOG

Lord, the pit of depression and sickness can leave me feeling old and worn out. You forgive me my sins, heal all my diseases and rescue me from the pit of depression. You crown me with mercy and compassion. You continually fill my life with so many blessings and renew my youth. I am strengthened and strong like an eagle. May my soul never forget all the good You have done.

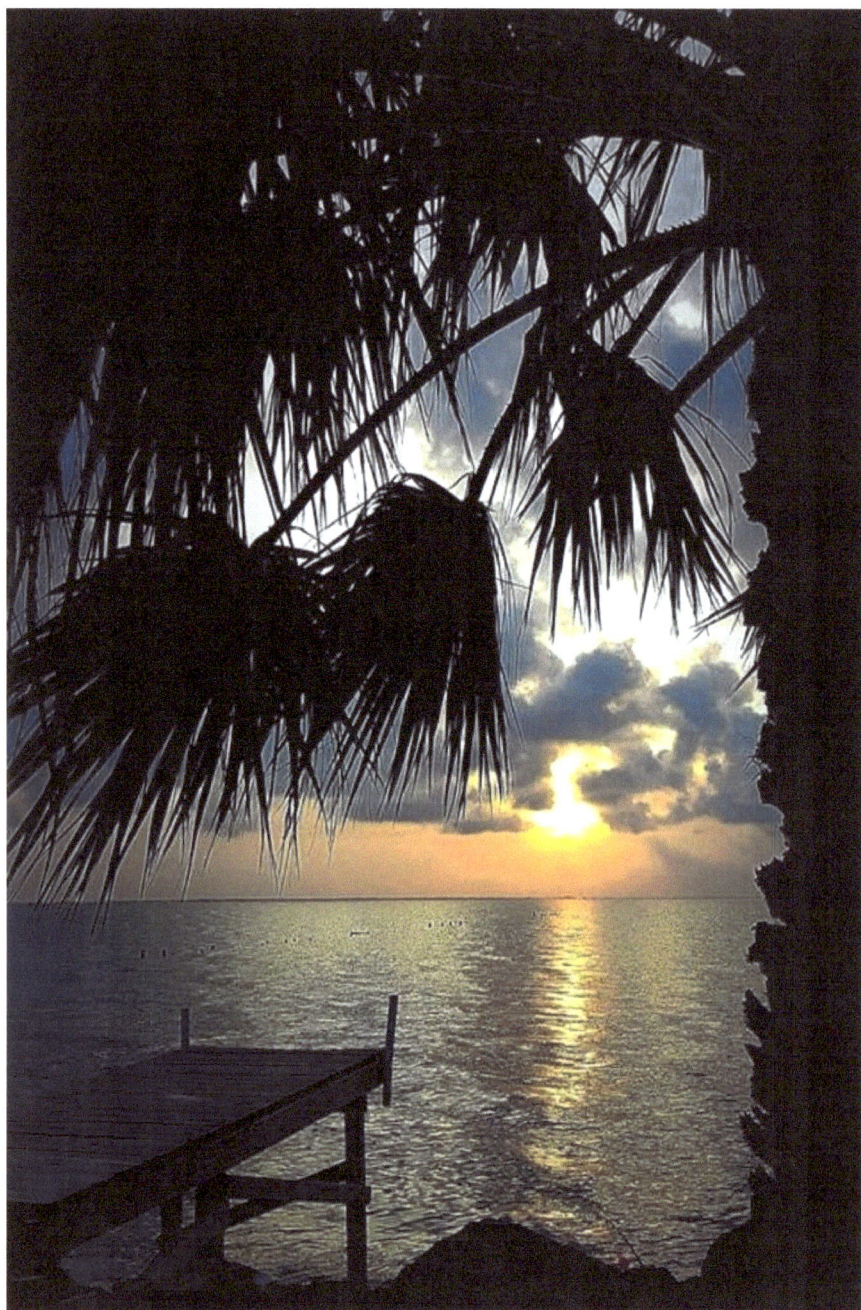

Twenty-Five

Pity me, O Lord, for I am weak. Heal me, for my body is sick.
~Psalm 6:2 TLB

Lord, I am not feeling it today. I am wanting a pity party and to wallow in my problems instead of walk out Your promises. Lord, strengthen and heal me today. May my pity be turned to praise.

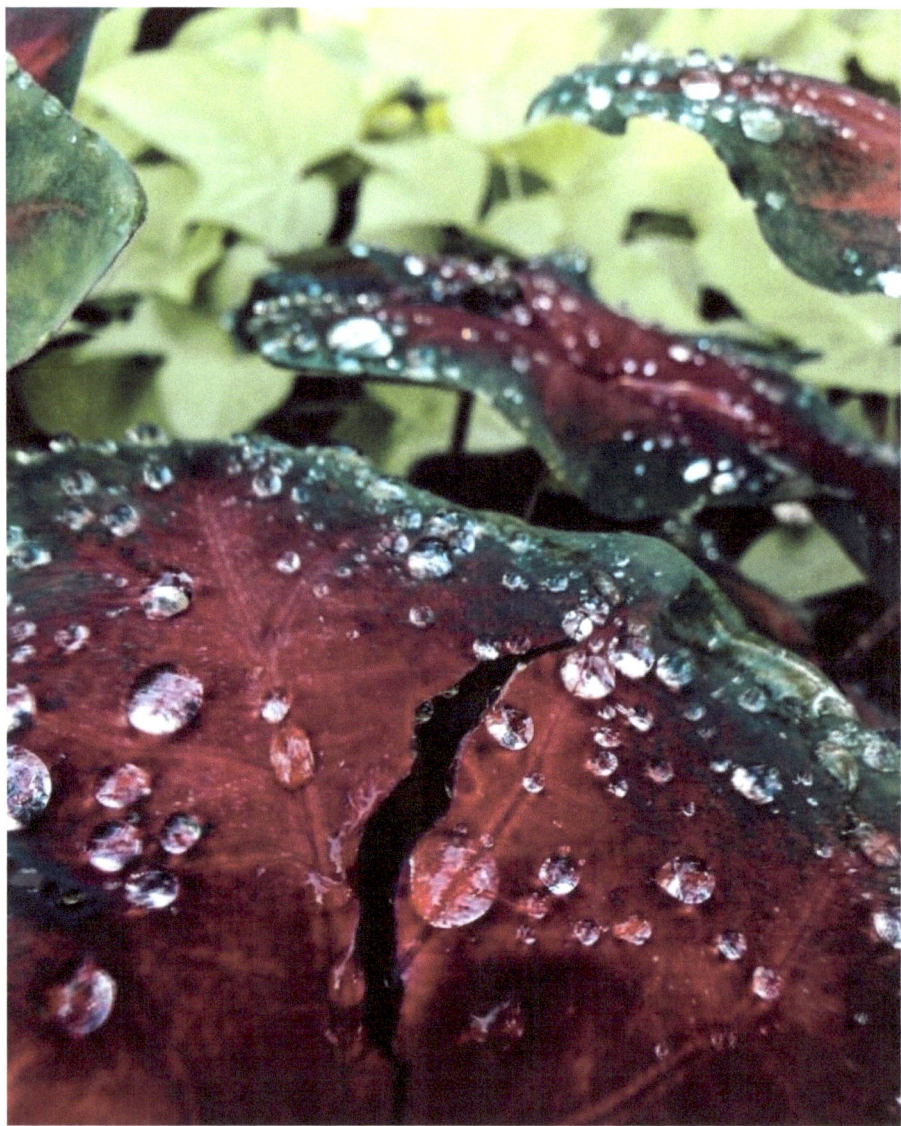

Twenty-Six

God is my bodyguard, shielding every bone; not even a finger gets broken.
~Psalm 34:20 MSG

As I go about my day Lord, thank You that I have the promise that You are my bodyguard. Thank You for shielding every bone in my body and that not even a finger will get broken. Thank You for your Divine Protection today and every day.

Twenty-Seven

After I have suffered for a little while, the God of all grace who imparts His blessing and favor, who called me to His own eternal glory in Christ, will Himself complete, confirm, strengthen, and establish me making me what I ought to be.
~1 Peter 5:10 AMP

Your Word never tells me I won't suffer. But Your Word does promise that You will impart blessing and favor and will not only heal me, but You promise to complete, confirm, strengthen and establish me. Lord, help me wait gracefully for Your promises to be fulfilled.

Twenty-Eight

God will wipe away all tears from my eyes, and there shall be no more death, nor sorrow, nor crying, nor pain. All of that has gone forever.
~Revelation 21:4 TLB

Lord, take away the pain. Wipe away all tears from my eyes. Thank You that You promise that all pain and tears, crying and sorrow will be gone forever.

Twenty-Nine

Not a single one of all the good promises that God has made went unfulfilled; all of them came to pass. ~Joshua 21:45 VOICE

You are not a God that lies. Your promises are always Yes and Amen. Not one goes unfulfilled. Lord, I am standing on Your Word believing that You will bring those promises to pass for me.

<u>Thirty</u>

With long life God will satisfy me and show me His salvation.
~Psalm 91:16 TLV

Lord, I will not listen to the fear of premature death. Your Word says that long life is what You promise.

Thirty-One

The Spirit of God, who raised Jesus from the dead, dwells in me. God who raised Christ from the dead will also give life to my mortal body through His Spirit who dwells in me.
~Romans 8:11 NKJV

My old life has been crucified with Christ, and I now live in the resurrection power. Christ's Spirit dwells within me and gives me life.

Photo Credits:

1 Little Reminders - Thomas Joel Trevino
2 Heart Hands Shadow - Joe & Connor Bollom
3 Serenity- Stephanie Richmond
4 Grand Canyon - Brittni Davis
5 Jesus Loves You - Thomas Joel Trevino
6 Mornings in The Word- Thomas Joel Trevino
7 Phi Phi Islands Ibiza Pool Thailand- Brittni Davis
8 What A View - Gülsün Gülduran
9 Windmill - Dennis Ramey
10 Butterfly - Wanda Foster
11 Morning Dew On Spider Web - Dennis Ramey
12 Fun In The Sun Rockport TX- Myranda Piña
13 Leaf - Gülsün Gülduran
14 Hamilton Pool Preserve - Thomas Joel Trevino
15 Endicott Bay Alaska - Brittni Davis
16 Reflecting - Thomas Joel Trevino
17 Snowy Trees - Igor Cancarevic / OVER app
18 Cat - Thomas Joel Trevino
19 Cavasso Creek- Dennis Ramey
20 Fishing - Dennis Ramey
21 Breakfast Capture - Thomas Joel Trevino
22 Silhouette Of Love - Thomas Joel Trevino
23 Fingernail Moon Rockport TX - Myranda Piña
24 Sailboats - Ismail Niyax / OVER app
25 Sunrise San Antonio Bay- Dennis Ramey
26 Dew Drops - Thomas Joel Trevino
27 Rockport Harbor - Connor Bollom
28 Snowy Central Park NYC - Myranda Piña
29 Christ Statue- Melissa Piña
30 Water Lilies - Melissa Piña
31 Changes Stockbridge, MA - Melissa Piña

Continue to pray the Word
with these books in the

Prayer Scripts Series

Your Rx for Fear
Your Rx for Overcoming Temptation
Your Rx for Forgiveness
Your Rx for Peace
Your Rx for Joy
Your Rx for Hope

For further encouragement, please visit
www.restoredministries.org
restoredministriesblog.wordpress.com
Facebook-Twitter-Instagram-You Tube

#LiveRestored
#MindBodySoul